SPIRITUAL WISDOM FOR PEACE ON EARTH FROM SANANDA CHANNELED THROUGH DAVID J ADAMS

DAVID ADAMS

authorHOUSE®

AuthorHouse™
1663 Liberty Drive
Bloomington, IN 47403
www.authorhouse.com
Phone: 1 (800) 839-8640

Published by AuthorHouse 04/16/2018

ISBN: 978-1-5462-3781-5 (sc)
ISBN: 978-1-5462-3779-2 (hc)
ISBN: 978-1-5462-3780-8 (e)

Library of Congress Control Number: 2018904460

Print information available on the last page.

Photo taken from the camera of David J Adams.

David Adams' T-shirt in front cover picture was created by Tie Dye Artist, Ruth Cary Cooper.

DEDICATION

I dedicate this book to my children, Nicky and Suzi, my grandchildren, Lauren, Matthew and Emily, and my great grandchildren, Ruby–Rae and Peyton, for they and others of the next generations will carry the Light forward and create the Peace that we all yearn for.

ABOUT THE AUTHOR

ADAMS, David John Patrick
Born: 28 April 1943

At: Mountain Ash, Glamorgan, South Wales, UK.

Lived 3 years in Karachi, Pakistan, and 2 years in Egypt, before moving to South Australia in 1971.

Currently living in the southern suburbs of the city of Adelaide.

Came to his path of awakening in late 1987, quite probably as a result of the energy of the Harmonic Convergence in August of that year.

Was quickly introduced to the beautiful world of Crystals, and joined a group called Crystal Consciousness - which shortly thereafter became "EarthMother" - under the leadership of Heather Niland.

In 1991, he was asked by Beloved Master Germain to undertake a global Meditation based on, and working with, the Consciousness of the Oceans, to be called the Marine Meditation. This was to be held at 8 pm on each Equinox wherever people were in the world. The Marine Meditation was held each Equinox from March 1991 to September 2012 – some 44 Meditations in all.

He continues to work both with Crystals and the Oceans. He attended a gathering of Masters in New Zealand in 1996, a healing Summit in Glastonbury, UK in 1998 and a healing Summit in South Molle, Queensland in 2000. In 2009 he was asked to address a Peace Conference in Istanbul to speak of the Marine Meditation and his work for World Peace through meditation.

David is a songwriter, a musician, a writer of Musical Theater productions and Author of the book "The Earthmother book of Energy based Healing" – now out of print. More important, David is a SERVANT OF PEACE.

He began bringing through information from a variety of Masters and Cosmic Beings in the form of Meditations around 1991, particularly a series of Meditations from the Spirit of Crystals and Gemstones. It was not, however, until after the year 2000 that he began to channel messages in group situations and in individual sessions. Most of these messages were not recorded or transcribed, and so most remain shared with only a few people. But in 2009 the messages being brought through in the weekly Pendragon Meditation group began to be recorded and transcribed by Kath Smith and sent out around the world on David's own Pendragon network. The disseminating of the audio versions of these messages did not begin until 2012.

David's special Guide and Mentor has been 'The Germain, the I am that I am', but he has also worked extensively with – and channeled - Sananda, Hilarion, Djwahl Khul, AA Michael, The Merlin, The Masters of Shambhala, as well as Arcturian Sound Master Tarak and his own Home Trinity Cosmic Brother Ar'Ak.

ACKNOWLEGEMENTS

I, David J Adams, would like to acknowledge three special Earth Angels.

Heather Niland/Shekina Shar -- who helped me awaken to my Journey in 1987 and connected me to my Beloved Friend "The Germain". She was a mentor, guide and teacher way ahead of her time.

Meredith Pope -- who walked in the same shoes as me in those difficult early years as a fellow 'weekender' at The EarthMother Center, and was, and still is, an inspiration to me.

Krista Sonnen – An Harmonic and Earthwalker who helped build the bridges to my Spiritual and Cosmic friends by persistently urging me to allow them to speak through me in private sessions, then in group sessions. Without her support, these messages would not be here.

I would further like to acknowledge **Kath Smith** -- A spiritual Being of immense Love and Joy who initiated the recording and transcribing of the messages received in Pendragon so the messages from our 'other Dimensional friends' would not be lost forever.

I also acknowledge all those here in Australia and those throughout the World who have supported me and encouraged me over the years, and in particular, **Barbara Wolf and Margaret Anderson**, who's vision and hard work has made this book possible.

BLESSINGS OF LOVE, JOY AND PEACE TO EACH AND EVERY ONE OF YOU.

DAVID J ADAMS

FOREWORD

The messages gifted from Beloved Sananda and contained in this book have the common theme of **PEACE**. Peace in the Heart and Peace on Earth.

It is my belief that Peace on Earth can - and will - be achieved through each individual finding Peace within the Heart, so I hope by reading Sananda's words you will begin to discover, embrace and nurture that energy of Peace within your own Heart and **SHARE IT WITH THE WORLD.**

LET PEACE PREVAIL.

INTRODUCTION

Back in 1992 I was gifted a series of meditations by an Energy Being that called itself "Spirit of Crystals and Gemstones". Each meditation was a 'Journey' with a specific crystal. One of these Crystals was 'Blue Lace Agate', and within the meditation we were taken on a journey to a distant Planet. A Planet where only **PEACE** and **LOVE** exist, wrapped in an atmosphere of serene blue.

We were told that *"This was once a Planet just like yours, filled with turmoil, anger, fear, hatred and war, until the Guardians came with their gift of Blue Light and offered an alternative to the total destruction that seemed such an inevitable consequence. Sit for a while and allow the essence of what this Planet has achieved to flow through every fiber of your Being. Feel the incredible depth of its serenity. It's a vibration unlike any you have experienced before. **TOTAL LOVE**.*

TOTAL PEACE. TOTAL SERENITY. Become ONE with that vibration."

The Guardian referred to was Sananda, Cosmic Ambassador of Peace, and he has been offering the gift of Blue Light to the Earth Planet through various 'Enlightened Beings' through the ages, beginning with 'The Christ' - which is why some believe that Sananda and 'The Christ' are one and the same. In more recent times Sananda has been offering the Blue Light of Peace directly to and through Beloved Earthmother. Earthmother has accepted the gift, but still requires that the majority of Humanity accept that gift, too. **These messages are a part of that process.**

I began directly channeling Sananda, Cosmic Ambassador of Peace, around the year 2000, at first in private sessions with my good friend and Harmonic Being Krista Sonnen, then later in an open meditation group. Most of the early channels were not recorded or transcribed so were only heard by those present at the time. The messages within this book are of more recent vintage, when the importance of the messages being received and their relevance to the wider Humanity was realized.

I hope they resonate within your Heart and lift you into the embrace of **PEACE.**

Blessings of Love and Peace

David J Adams

CONTENTS

1

MESSAGE FROM SANANDA
September 12, 2002

At this particular time your Planet is filled with thoughts of war, of revenge, of conflict. It is therefore of vital importance that each individual looks within their own Hearts to find the 'Energies of Peace' that have been planted there to focus their Light on these 'Energies of peace' to expand them through their hearts, to expand them through their Beings. To radiate the 'Energies of peace' powerfully, more powerfully than ever before.

BALANCE IS IMPORTANT. All Global decisions need to be made in a state of Balance. There are no right or wrong decisions, there are merely decisions and consequences of decisions. To ensure that important decisions are made in Balance, 'Energies of Peace' need to be as powerful as the energies of war, the energies of fear. It is most important when you come to your Marine Meditation... MORE THAN EVER... to fill your Oceans with LOVE, with JOY and with PEACE. Consciously we ask you to place it in your minds as well as in your hearts, DAILY to think of PEACE. Think of it perhaps as your BLUE LIGHT. Perhaps as your MAGENTA LIGHT from the CRYSTAL OF DIVINE PEACE, perhaps as the Peace that comes with your PINK LIGHT of LOVE. Whichever Light you wish to work with, DO SO POWERFULLY!... see it permeating the Earth, see it permeating every Being on the Earth, Know that YOUR LIGHT is where it all begins, so LET YOUR LIGHT OF PEACE SHINE.

Draw more powerfully through your special Crystal from The Blue Planet, ask for those 'Energies of Peace' to be drawn into your Being that you might radiate them forth. LOVE WILL PREVAIL, Dear Ones, PEACE WILL PREVAIL. But as you were warned in the message for the Marine Meditation, you will not necessarily like all that comes to light at this time, do not allow yourselves to be drawn back into fear... and that is one aspect of your 11 Sept anniversary... yes it is time to honor those that sacrificed themselves, but it is also an opportunity for some to create fear, to create it once more… and that needs to be balanced, balanced with the PURE 'Energies of Peace'. It is easy to lose sight of the bigger picture when your screens are filled with images which deliberately utilize and create the maximum of fear. But it doesn't matter how it is portrayed, the world didn't come to an end on the 11th Sept last year. It will not come to an end now. Work with PEACE, work with LOVE, work with JOY. Do not focus on the negatives, do not focus on the fear, do not give that your strength. Respond always by drawing more powerfully on the Love and Peace and Joy in your own Heart. RESPOND WITH YOUR LIGHT.

Many Cosmic Beings are here at this time, draw them into your circle, join with them in PEACE and HARMONY. There are many Sacred Circles, indeed there are many Circles. The power of the Circle is the composite of all within it. If all within it are in PEACE and LOVE, then indeed you have a SACRED CIRCLE.

Imagine your Medicine Wheel spinning and spinning, sending forth shafts of Light containing PEACE, containing JOY, containing LOVE, and know that these are at work even though the images on your screens do not tell you this. YOU KNOW THAT IT IS SO!!!

We are looking forward to your Marine Meditation with great joy. Your ocean friends are also working diligently at this time to create the 'Energies of Peace' within their environment. It will be indeed a powerful voice that sounds forth your Joy.

It is important to remind people that they do have the CHOICE OF PEACE! they do have the CHOICE OF LOVE, they do have the CHOICE OF JOY... when all they see in front of them is fear... THEY ALWAYS HAVE THOSE CHOICES!! There are alternatives, there are other choices people can make... sometimes you get so overwhelmed with one idea, you do not see past that, you do not see the choices you have... but if you look into your own Heart... THE CHOICE OF LOVE IS ALWAYS THERE!

Blessings

Sananda

2

MESSAGE FROM SANANDA

July 12, 2010

Greetings Beloveds, I am Sananda, Ambassador of Peace in the Cosmos. I come to you tonight, briefly, to speak to you about the need to continue your work for Peace throughout the World. The significance of July 11th (*Full Lunar Eclipse on a New Moon*) can not be overstated, it was and is a powerful time of change on your planet, an opportunity, a closure of one Cycle and the opening of another.

Over the past month in your time, you have witnessed the expression of the Cosmos through Sound, broadcast across your Earth from the World cup. On July 11th that came to an end. A whole month of Planetary Sound reflected and magnified through this great coming together on your planet. You may therefore feel that it is time to sit back, that all is now done, but of course, Dear Ones, it is only just beginning.

The Sound of the Grand Cross has reverberated around your Earth, cleansing, purifying, sometimes annoying, but then sometimes it takes an energy that annoys to awaken Souls who are in some respect solidified in your third Dimensional frequencies.

Sound shakes, Sound confronts, and people have been asked to move beyond that and to embrace what is beneath the surface of the Sound. The energies of Joy, the energies of Connection, of coming together as **ONE** across your world.

For although the World Cup as you call it, is by nature a competition, it is also a time of bringing people together. It was not by accident that the last event at which this Sound was heard was allowed to go longer than scheduled, to give that extra bit of impetus to the Sound frequencies as they rolled across the Earth. This Sound of Joy, this Sound of **ONENESS**, prepares the Earth for the energies of Peace and Love incarnate within the 5th Dimension that you will rapidly move into.

Some of you are already working within that Dimension, and are often spaced out or at least give that appearance to others. Do not let that concern you. Focus on what you need to focus on, which is the **NOW** moment. The **NOW** moment is creating your tomorrows. The **NOW** moment is shedding your past. The **NOW** moment **IS LOVE, PEACE** and **JOY**.

The powerful Planetary alignments will continue to impact upon the Earth, and upon all those upon and within the Earth for many months to come, for these are all slow moving Planets, they do not come and go in the blink of an eye. They move slowly, and their energy is powerful. Harness that energy within your Heart. Focus on **PEACE**, Focus on **LOVE**. To do this you will need to change your perceptions and to become aware, much more aware, of what it is that you are being shown at this time. Many of you will watch your news broadcasts and you will see only what you are being allowed to see by those who have vested interests in creation emotions, emotions to bind you, emotions to hold you imprisoned in lower Dimensional frequencies. You do not deal with these by ignoring them, you deal with these by being aware of what is behind what you are seeing. You give your love and compassion to those who need it, but you do not allow yourself to become sucked in to those emotions that you are being asked to adopt.

There are wars all around your Planet, all are given noble motives but all are still wars. Be aware that they exist, but do not lend them energy, give them instead, Peace and Love.

Each time you are confronted by a situation which is designed specifically to tug at your Heart strings, and this is done in a myriad of ways, Dear Ones, not only in Human stories, but in animal stories and through stories of Earth destruction – all these things are designed specifically to tug at your Heart strings – Be aware of this, Dear Ones, give Peace and give Love and do not give judgments to perpetrators, or to those seeking to control the media of your world. There is no benefit to be obtained by being judgmental, for it is not their fault if **YOU** choose to become embroiled in those emotions.

Remember, Dear Ones, **YOU** are in control of your emotions, **YOU** choose your own reactions to whatever you are faced with in this life. Let go of blame, let go of judgment, accept totally **YOUR** choice to create delight and the world that **YOU** want. You do this, Dear Ones, by simply being aware of what others are seeking to do to your emotions, and make **YOUR** choices based on what is within your Heart, and not what is within your television screens.

The time of **"SOUND"** has finished for this moment, but it will come again, for there is much more to be done as the next period of time on your Planet moves quickly through Dimensional frequencies. It behooves you to remain **CENTERED** within your Hearts, not **Earthed** within your Planet, but **CENTERED** within your Hearts, for it is within your Hearts that you will be guided into all the new Dimensional frequencies.

I thank you for listening to me, I am Sananda, and I bless you all.

Let us focus our attention on the planet as a whole. Connect deeply with your heart to the heart of the planet, feel the peace and the love and the Joy bursting from every seam of the Planet, raging through every grid upon the Planet, singing a song of the New Earth, a song of Love, a song of Joy, a song of Peace. Let your Heart sing also.

Let Peace prevail.

So be it.

3

RIDE THE WAVE OF LOVE ENERGIES INTO THE HIGHER DIMENSIONAL FREQUENCIES

June 13, 2011

Allow yourselves to embrace the totality of your Being. Expand your consciousness, to embrace the multidimensionality of your Being.

Beloved ones, I greet you, I am Sananda. It is important to realize at this time, that what you call the brain, is simply a mechanism for operating in the dimension that you now exist. It is, if you like, the custodian of all that has been in this current life, a storeroom of memories - everything you have ever heard, you have ever seen, you have ever read, you have ever experienced, is housed within this brain.

You brain does not connect you beyond this dimension. It is your heart which allows you to connect to the Akashic records, which store the memories of past existences. Your brain is purely for this lifetime. Once you recognize and acknowledge this fact, you will look afresh at what you are being asked to do by Spirit. You are being asked to let go of old paradigms, of old ways of thinking and feeling, in order to bring into existence the New Earth, and you will realize that the brain cannot create the New Earth, other than by recasting that which is in its memory.

That is not creating something new, it is reconstituting something that is old, giving a "face lift" to the past, but Ascension is not about giving a "face lift" to the past, it is about opening to a totally new perception, a totally new Earth that comes from the heart, comes from your soul - **for you are moving out of a dimension of flesh, and into a dimension of Spirit.** The vibrational frequencies of the higher dimensions will create something beyond that which your brain can conceive. Your brain will always recreate in different forms, aspects of your past, for that is all that it knows.

So when Spirit says to you – "let go of the past" – it is asking you to open your heart to something completely new. It is not asking you to let go of isolated incidents of your past that may have, within your lifetime, created disharmony for you. It is asking you to shift your attention from your brain into your heart, and to allow the Divine energy of Love to open new awareness, new understanding, new acceptance of what is to come.

Everything you have experienced within this lifetime has brought you to this place of change. It is now time to let go of the outmoded methods of the past, to move deeply into your hearts, and **through your hearts ride the wave of love energies into the higher dimensional frequencies,** and within those frequencies you will find visions of the Cosmos and the Beings of Light within the Cosmos, that your brain is incapable of understanding at this time.

Do this by honoring what your brain has been for you in this life time - a custodian of all that you have created. Honor it, then move into the higher vibrational frequencies of your heart, and feel the doors opening into these higher dimensional frequencies.

The Ascended Masters, the Cosmic Masters all await you; all reach out to embrace you in the new energy of Divine Love, of Infinite Light, of True Harmony.

Take a moment now to sit within the comfort of your own heart space. Imagine if you like, that you are sitting in the auditorium of a cinema, and on the screen your brain is replaying all the events of your life. View them with detachment, acknowledge their worth, and give them the love that they deserve, for you are honoring one stage of a journey, that has had many stages, and you are preparing to move forward into the next stage of your journey of Love and Light.

Imagine you are being surrounded with Blue Light, the Blue Light of Infinite Peace, filling you with deep, deep Serenity, that allows you to let go, that allows you to move on.

This is a time of transition, for you as individual Beings of Light upon this Planet and transition of beloved Earth Planet itself, into the Higher Realms of Divine Love, Divine Peace.

Allow the energies of Love and Peace to be expressed through your Heart, through your voice, through your souls, embracing all that has been, all that is, and all that is to be.

Honor and give thanks for all you have experienced within this lifetime.

Give blessings to all who have contributed to your journey of Love, your journey of Light, your journey into Oneness.

I embrace you with Love and Peace. Blessings be upon you.

4

SHINE YOUR LIGHT OF UNITY – BE THE BEACONS FOR OTHERS

October 3, 2011

(The meditation circle sounds Tibetan bowls.)

Feel those waves of sound opening your Heart chakra totally and completely, accepting the inflow of Light from the Earth itself, from the Cosmos, from all your Guides and friends, and feel yourself becoming enriched and empowered by this infusion of Divine Light.

As you open your Hearts to this Light, open your Consciousness to the Lights of all other Consciousnesses within the Universe, embracing and accepting that we are all part of the **ONE**. Look beyond the images that flow into your eyes. See and feel the images that come into your Heart - images of wisdom and understanding - images of acceptance.

We have moved through the Portal of Transformation, and reside now within the Consciousness of Unity – Unity with all Beings of Light, from whatever source, and in whatever form, connecting deeply and personally with the Light within each consciousness, for **it is through the Light that we come into oneness, into Unity with the Creator.**

It is time to let go of your memories of your time of separation, to begin to identify yourself with the whole.

Your lives on this place and in other places have been part of a single journey of expanding Consciousness.

Along that journey you have taken many forms, and you have been to many places, but they are all a part of the one journey – the journey into Divine Love.

You will continue to exist in a dimension which is filled with separateness, for that is still the perception of many on your Planet.

The purpose for you, however, is to remain steadfast in your oneness, to observe and acknowledge the perceptions of others, but not to judge those perceptions, or allow yourselves to be drawn back into those perceptions.

It's time to shine your Light of Unity, to be the beacons for others.

As you look out upon your Dimension, look beyond the physical, look into the Consciousness of all that is, and you will find a greater affinity with all that is around you. Embrace that affinity, share your Light, attract their Light, be **ONE WITH ALL THAT IS.**

Focus now on the Light within your Heart, not as an individual, independent Light, but as part of the Light of all creation - and feel yourself empowered, uplifted, enhanced in every way.

Allow your Light to flow outwards into the world - embracing all - judging none.

Beloved ones, I am Sananda, and I come here tonight to bless you for taking these steps into the Consciousness of Unity. We are indeed all ONE.

Blessings be.

5

LOVE SIMPLY IS THE ENERGY AND THE ESSENCE OF SOURCE

February 6, 2012

(The meditation circle opens with the sounds of the Tibetan bowls and the crystal bowl and chimes.)

Allow the resonance of those Sound vibrations to loosen any remaining vestiges of shadows within your Being, letting go of all that is of fear, and replacing it with pure Light, that your whole Being may be Enlightened completely.

Greetings Beloveds, I am Sananda, Ambassador of Peace from the Cosmos.

When you came to this place at the beginning of time, you came filled with Divine Light, and with the energy of pure Divine Unconditional Love.

As you created your world of duality, you allowed the energies of Love to subside in your density, and move from the embrace of your Heart Chakra down into the Spleen Chakra, where it became a part of your duality – "love and hate", "fear and love" – competing for space, and Love became just another commodity to serve your learning in the density and the duality.

Each time you moved from this place, and then returned, you came anew with the Divine Unconditional Love.

As you look into the eyes of a babe, you will see no fear. You will see no hate. You will see only the Divine Unconditional Love energy until, in time, the density that you have created once more snuffs out the Divine Unconditional Love.

Once again it becomes a 'currency' in your relationships. It is the game that you have chosen to play for eons of time in each and every life time. You bring with you that gift of Pure Unconditional Love, then you shift it downwards into the density and into your Spleen Chakra.

You may ask "why is it important to speak of this now?" Well as we have been telling you for some time – **it is now time to let go of old belief systems, old paradigms, old methodologies that were acceptable in the time of denseness and duality, but are no longer relevant in the new world of Love and Light and Oneness.**

It is time to begin the process, if you have not already started that process, of lifting that energy of Love back from your Spleen Chakra, up into your Heart Chakra, where once again it will be pure - almost innocent - but powerful as a guiding force in your lives.

You have been asked by **Beloved Germain** to look at the World through your Heart. To do that effectively you need to lift the energy of Love back into your Heart, and let it go from your Spleen, for **the energy of Love is not an emotional response in the New World as it was in the old.** It is not a carrot and a stick, as it was in the old world.

The new Earth will be pure of Love and pure of Light, so it is time to let go of those aspects of your existence that no longer serve **YOU** in the New Earth energies.

It is time to redefine the word "Love" in your minds.

It is time to let go of the 'emotion' that you have called Love previously, and to work with the pure "Energy of Love".

The energy of Love is not unidirectional as the emotion is. It is not about person to person. **It is about a contract between you and all that is - everyone, every Being on this Earth, every creature on this Earth.** You are capable of embracing with Love - **Pure Unconditional Love.**

In the past you have treated Love as a currency, almost like your bank account, and you have carefully monitored the inflow and the outflow to ensure that you are in balance, or better still, in profit. But Love is none of those – **Love simply is the energy and the essence of Source.**

As you embrace the pure energy of Love within your Hearts, and allow that to shine forth and embrace all those around you, and all those around the Earth - you will release yourselves from the shackles of the past.

You will feel within yourself a new sense of freedom.

The reality Dear Ones, is that you have not been enslaved by others, you have enslaved yourselves! but that time is over.

It is time to be free, to be free to show your Love for 'ALL THAT IS'.

Take a moment to simply sit within your Heart and feel the purity of the Love Energy, unencumbered by the debts of the past. The shackles fall away, and a new lightness takes possession of your Being, and you look out upon the World in a totally different way.

For when you sit within the Energy of Love - you feel and see yourself in a different way - no longer a slave to the emotional rollercoaster of your life - peaceful, calm, harmonious, enlightened.

Feel how joyful that is, how much your body resonates anew to the sound of Love.

I ask you to focus daily when you arise from your sleep, on the "Energy of Love", and allow that to

flow from you as you move through your daily tasks.

Let your Light shine strongly.

Do not concern yourself unduly with the reactions of others, simply **BE** the Light and Love that you are, and you will change the World simply by being in the Energy of Love.

I bless and thank you for sharing your special Light with me this evening.

I embrace you with the deepest Love in my Heart.

6

ACKNOWLEDGE YOURSELF AS A BEING OF PURE LOVE

June 4, 2012

(The meditation circle opens with the sounds of the Tibetan bowls and the chimes.)

Allow the vibrations of the bowls to open all your chakras, bringing them into alignment - into the wholeness of your Being. Feel the frequency of the sound uplift you into your Soul Heart.

Greeting Beloveds, **I am Sananda - Cosmic Ambassador of Peace**, and I come to you at this time to speak to you of Peace, for the Earth Planet is now moving into a time of intense Cosmic activity. Great energies from the Great Central Sun are cascading down upon your Earth Planet at this time. **The energies of Divine Love as heralded by the**

Venus Transit, are caressing the Earth and all upon it.

As with all Cosmic energies, it is important to embrace them, and then give them purpose – by focusing those energies on specific areas of your lives, on specific elements of the Earth, and at this time, when you are bathed in the Light of Divine Love, I ask you to focus these energies on activating the essences of Peace upon the Earth.

As we have indicated to you before, from the beginning of time on your Planet the special energies of Divine Peace were encapsulated at various points on your Planet - in your Pyramids of Peace. Now is the time for those Pyramids to become activated through the Divine Love of the Cosmos, through the Divine Love embraced and focused through your Hearts.

It is time to call into being - for the whole of the Earth Planet- the energies of Divine Peace, to allow those energies to permeate all aspects of life upon the Earth Planet, by focusing the Divine Love energies into the Blue Light of Peace, and connecting this Blue Light of Peace from within your Heart, to the

Hearts of all others upon the Earth, for **Peace is a very specific energy**.

It is more than the cessation of hostilities; it is the energy that allows you to live the Love that is within your Hearts. The energy of Love cannot be shared within anger or fear or hostility. It grows within the energies of Peace.

Peace and Love are two sides of the same coin. They are linked intrinsically in all aspects of the Earth and all aspects of the Beings of Light upon the Earth.

The powerful energies that are now flowing into the Planet need to be focused, and that is your role as **'change makers'** upon the Earth, to accept and embrace the energies of the Great Central Sun, and to focus them.

As you look out onto the Earth - not just upon your fellow humans, but upon all creatures, upon all of nature - do so with the focus of Divine Love and Divine Peace radiating from your Heart, your Heart which is no longer contained within the limitations of your physical vessel, your Heart that is expanded and embraces all.

For you have embraced your relationship with the whole, with all that is.

This is indeed a time of great change upon the Earth, and you will receive many inflows of energy throughout the remainder of this linear year of your time. Each will build upon the one before, but all will be filtered through your Soul Hearts.

I invite you now to feel these energies as they flow from the Cosmos as an upsurge of joyfulness within you, eradicating all the old fears, all the old anger and hatred of the past.

Embrace fully the energies that are cascading into you, and onto you, and through you at this time.

None of these energies are for the purpose of hurting others, or you. Embrace them fully then focus them, shine forth your Blue Light of Peace that others may be empowered to shine forth their Light, to discover within themselves the capacity for Love and Peace.

As you work diligently with these powerful Cosmic energies, feel pure Joy.

It is time for each and every one of you to reach into your Hearts, to turn up the light within you, and allow that Love to shine forth, acknowledge yourself as a Being of Pure Love.

I embrace you all with the Blue Light of Peace from the Great Central Sun, and ask you to carry it forth and breathe that Blue Light out into the world, to allow the changes to take place in a balanced and harmonious way.

7

I BLESS YOU AND EMBRACE YOU WITH THE BLUE MIST OF PEACE

October 29, 2012

(The Circle opens with the sounds of the Tibetan bowls.)

Greetings Dear Hearts, I am Sananda, Cosmic Ambassador of Peace.

As many of you will know, this one through whom I speak tonight operates within the vibration of the number 8, in fact it may be perceived as his own vibration, so it will come as no great surprise to you when I mention that it was 8 years ago in 2004 that I came to this Circle and offered to your Hearts the gift of the Pyramid of Divine Peace for you to spin, spin, spin and radiate the energies of the Blue Light of Peace.

Later that same year I came a second time and offered you another Pyramid of Peace to link with the first Pyramid and create a Diamond of Peace within your Hearts, radiating a Gold Light, and this enabled you to work more powerfully with the Diamond Labyrinth that you walked in 2005.

On the 8th of the 8th in 2005 I came for a third time and offered you the gift of the Crystal of Divine Peace, in the form of an 8 pointed star to sit between your Heart and your Thymus, connecting the Peace in your Heart to the Peace within your Soul through your Higher Heart frequencies. This again empowered you as you walked the 8 Pointed Star Labyrinth of 2006. Now Dear Hearts on this 8 vibration day I come to you again with a gift of Peace.

A short while ago this one, David, and the one called Kath - who facilitates these messages going out from this Circle to the rest of the World - were taken on a journey to the Centre of the Cosmos, to the Home Planet of this one (David) - the Planet of YRDD - a Planet of Peace, and there they were offered the **Pure Light of Peace from the Creator**, and as they accepted this gift they were filled with the "Blue Mist of Peace" that permeated every aspect of their Being, every aspect of their multi-dimensional Beings. Then they were returned to the Earth Planet.

It has taken some time for those higher frequency Peace energies to become harmonized within them, but now that has taken place and we are ready, **together** as a **Trinity of Peace,** to offer each and every one of you the gift of this '**Pure Light of Peace', not only those of you who are in this Circle tonight but those who may be reading this message or listening to this message, for you are all part of the ONE and you are all with us now in this moment, in the 'NOW' moment, participating.**

So I will ask David and Kath to join me in a 'Trinity of Peace' to gift to each of you tonight the Pure Peace energies from the Creator. We will do this by asking you to stand between us and we will join hands in a Trinity, and place one hand against your Crown Chakra, and the other at your High Heart Chakra. As this is a Dimension of free will, we will ask you first if you are open to receiving this gift of the pure Light of Peace, and if you are, you will say so, and we will gift it to you.

So I ask now that David and Kath join with me.
(Sananda, David and Kath then move to each person in the circle.)

We ask you Dear one to stand between us.

"Are you open to receiving the pure Light of Peace? - I am.

As our hands are placed upon you, we ask you to sense, feel, and vision that from our hands there is a Mist of Blue Light moving into your body, moving into your energy body, and moving into your multidimensional Being, filling you completely with the Pure Light of Peace from the Creator.

Feel, sense, vision the Mist of Blue Light."

We ask you now to resume your seat.

We ask you to rise and stand between us, and we ask

"Are you open to receiving the Pure Light of Peace? – I am.

We place our hands on your Crown Chakra and your High Heart Chakra, and ask you to feel and sense and vision the Mist of Blue Light flowing from this Trinity of Peace into every aspect of your body, every aspect of your energy body, and every aspect of your multidimensional Being, filling you completely.

Feel, sense, and vision the Mist of Blue Light filling you."

We ask you now to resume your seat.

We ask you to stand between us.

"Are you open to receive the Pure Light of Peace? – I certainly am.

We place our hands on your Crown Chakra and your High Heart Chakra and ask you to feel, sense, and vision the Mist of Blue Light flowing from our hands deep into your body, filling your physical body, filling your energy body, filling your multidimensional Being.

Feel, sense, and vision the Mist of Blue Light flowing to you and through you."

We ask you now to resume your seat.

We ask that you stand between us.

"Are you open to receiving the Pure Light of Peace? – I am.

"We place our hands on your Crown Chakra and your High Heart Chakra and ask that you feel, sense and vision the Mist of Blue Light flowing through our hands to fill your physical body, to fill your energy body, to fill your multidimensional Being.

Feel, sense, vision the Mist of Blue Light flowing to you and through you."

We ask you now to resume your seat.

(Sananda acknowledges, honors and blesses THE TRINITY OF PEACE.)

I thank David and I thank Kath for agreeing to be part of the Trinity of Peace, to deliver the Pure Light of Peace from the Creator to each and every one of you present, and each and every one of you participating in the now moment, in the Dimension of Oneness.

It will take some time for these energies to become harmonized and aligned within your physical vessels, your energy vessels and your multidimensional Beings, but when that harmonization occurs you will **know** immediately within your **Heart**, and you will feel the upliftment of Peace on a level you have never imagined before, **and <u>at that time</u> I invite you to share that Pure Light of Peace with others in the same way that we have shared it tonight.**

You may call upon my energy, the energy of your Guide or your particular favorite Master to create a Trinity of Peace to work with someone else, for the Light of Peace is moving rapidly towards the earth planet, and you are the way showers once more, you are the anchors of the energies of Peace.

There are many steps along the pathway to Illumination and Enlightenment. There are many steps along the pathway to Ascension, and there are many steps on the pathway to the New Earth, and you will each walk this pathway at your own pace and in your own time, **for although you are walking the same path, it is never in the same shoes.**

So do not compare yourself with others, simply embrace who you are, what you are and where you are on your journey.

Dear Hearts, I bless you and embrace you with the **Blue Mist of Peace**.

8

SELF-LOVE ALLOWS YOU TO LOVE OTHERS

January 21, 2013

(The Circle opens with the sounds of the Tibetan bowls and the Tingsha Bells.)

Allow the Sounds of the bowls to flood your Being with the vibrations of Light. Feel yourself being uplifted on the waves of Light and Love, and allow those vibrations of Sound to flow from your Being out across the Earth, to create the energies of upliftment for all who are waiting to receive them, **for many more people are waiting at this time for the energies of upliftment to come into their Consciousness.**

Their Hearts are open, even when their minds are closed, so radiate forth the vibrations of Love and Light from deep within **your** Heart, and speak to **their** Hearts, for in the New Earth frequencies communication will be from Heart to Heart, for your Heart knows the reality of your existence, and even though the mind continues to play in the arena of illusion, your Heart now communicates, one with the other in true reality.

The shift that has recently taken place upon the Earth has opened the Hearts of every Being upon your Planet - not only humanity, but **ALL** Beings on your Planet, so as you resonate forth the energies of Love, you are communicating with every other Being on the Earth, and you are empowering every other Being on the Earth, **by allowing their Hearts to know that ALL is now possible,** that **ALL** is now moving in a new frequency, a new enlightenment, and from the inside out changes will take place in each Being, and through each Being, and those changes will be reflected in the outer world, **for the energy of Love can no longer be stifled or suppressed by the fear of the past, for the fear is the illusion, and Love is the reality.**

Each and every one of you will have a different role to play in creating this new world of Love. None is greater than the other, you simply all have a price to pay, **and that price is Love.** Gift it openly, honestly, do not hold back. You do not seek to command others how they receive those energies or what they do with those energies, you simply radiate them forth knowing that in doing so, you are creating the New Earth - **a place of Unity, a place of Harmony, a place of Serenity.**

Take a moment now to move deep within your Hearts and beat the drum, **the drum of Love**, and send out the vibrations of Love on your drum beats, pulsing them out into the world, and also be open yourselves to receive those drum beats from others into your Heart, for this is no longer giving and receiving, **this is sharing. It is being part of the flow - the flow of Love.** Each one supporting and empowering the other, so that **TOGETHER** you create a World of Love, and as you feel yourself filling with the energies of Love, you become more joyful, you feel a happiness you have never experienced before, and in that happiness there can only be Peace and Harmony.

Do not sit back Dear Ones and wait for someone else to create the changes of the Earth. Accept your full responsibility for being a part of those changes, of being a part of the vibration of Love.

Self-Love allows you to Love others. Embrace the Love and the Light of ALL.

Dear Ones, I am Sananda and I come often to speak with you of Peace, but Peace cannot exist in your world until Love takes over, and the great shift that has recently taken place has opened the door to allow **you** to find the Love in your Hearts, and to **share** the Love in your Hearts, and **when you share that Love, you create the energies of Peace,** and the Blue Mist of Peace will move on that vibration of Love across the Earth, and you will begin to see the changes taking place in your outer world, to match the changes that have already taken place in your inner world.

Beloved Germain has asked you to **"BE love in all you say and all you do"**, and if you accept that challenge, you will also be creating **Peace on Earth**.

Blessings be upon you.

9

PEACE WILL PREVAIL
April 8, 2013

(Meditation Circle.)

Greetings, Dear Hearts, I am Sananda, Cosmic Ambassador of Peace.

You may feel as you look around your Earth at this time, that Peace is a complete illusion, that we have spoken of Peace and Harmony coming to the Earth Planet but only chaos, anger and hatred seem to be in evidence at this time. But let me assure you, Dear Ones, that **Peace is moving swiftly into the Hearts of ALL upon the Earth Planet, but as Peace moves in, what is already in existence within those Hearts must be moved out!** so what you are seeing as you look around your Earth - at the anger and the hatred - is an **exodus of the old energies from the Hearts of Humanity!**

We have spoken to you often about the need to release old energies, and you have experienced over the last number of years how instances from your past have been brought to the surface once more for you to look at, bless, and release, and this is what is happening on an Earth basis at this time.

The old orders of corruption, of control, are being lifted to the surface for all to see, for all to recognize, and for all to transmute with the Divine Love energies that are growing deep within the Hearts of ALL upon the Earth.

There are many, of course, who do not recognize this transition of energies, but **YOU** as light workers should know that this is what is occurring.

Peace is truly taking root upon the Earth, and all those energies which are not of Peace, and not of Harmony are being expunged from the fabric of your societies, and that, Dear Hearts, is why you are seeing so much of these seemingly negative energies at this time. **They are all being lifted into the awareness of Humanity so that they may be released.**

But of course, at times like this it is so easy to be drawn back into the emotions of those energies, and this Dear Hearts is where the discernment of which we have spoken frequently comes into play.

Look out across your Earth and see these manifestations of negative energies, but **do not fall into them**, simply recognize that they are being lifted up into your awareness to allow you finally to release them.

Each individual needs to draw to the surface of their lives the anger, the pain, the negative energies within themselves and release **them**, and of course your communication media focuses very much on these negative energies, and that is how it should be Dear Ones.

It is important for each person upon the Earth to see what has been, and to recognize that it no longer needs to be! - that when you allow the Love, the Divine Love to fill your Hearts until there is no room for anger, there is no room for hatred, and it disintegrates from the surface of your mind, and as the Divine Love fills your Hearts, you begin to understand precisely what Peace really is.

Peace has never been just the absence of war; Peace has been and will be a complete acceptance of the equality of ALL upon your planet.

Sit for a moment and try to imagine a world where __ALL__ are accepted by __ALL__ - __ALL__ are embraced by __ALL__ - __ALL__ are Loved - __ALL__ are in Peace.

Can you feel the upliftment of your Soul as you imagine that? BUT that is not a dream Dear Hearts, it is your reality -<u>when you are ready to create that reality</u> - and that time Dear Hearts is NOW.

So, as you see the residual negative energies being brought to the surface, bless them, and let them go, and move deep within your Hearts and surround yourself with the Divine Love that resides in that place.

<u>PEACE WILL PREVAIL</u>

Blessing be upon you Dear Hearts.

10

ONE WITH ALL UPON THE EARTH, ONE WITH ALL THROUGHOUT THE COSMOS

July 15, 2013

(The circle opens with the Sounds of the Tibetan Bowls and the Blessings Chimes.)

Feel yourselves being lifted up into the higher dimensional frequencies by the sound of the bowls and the Blessings Chimes. Feel yourself expanding, drawing into your Heart **all that is around you** - All the Beings of Light that are sharing this gathering with you tonight. Bring them all into your Heart, and as you feel the power of their Light within you, expand even further, and draw into your Heart all the Beings of Light around the Earth. Feel the pulsation of **THEIR** Light becoming **ONE** with the pulsations of Light from deep within your

Heart. **Feel the Oneness, feel its power, feel its tenderness, for Love is both tender and powerful.**

Expand yourselves even more and embrace all the Light Beings of the Cosmos, drawing them into your Heart, feeling their pulsations of Light within you, feeling the Oneness grow and grow, for this, Dear Ones, is who you truly are, **One with all upon the Earth, One with all throughout the Cosmos, and it is time to embrace the complete Oneness, and no longer isolate yourself from others, no longer separate yourself. Feel the true power of YOU.**

Beloved Ones, I am Sananda, Ambassador of Peace and I come tonight to thank you for the service that you have recently conducted at the sacred place you call Willow Springs, where you came together in your Hearts and allowed **the Blue Light of Peace from the Cosmos to marry completely with the Blue Wave of Harmony from the center of the Heart of the Earth,** drawing together these powerful, powerful rays of Blue Light into a single unified column of Peace and Harmony, and then as you asked - **as you commanded** - this fusion of Blue Light to flow throughout the Earth, through the Song Lines of the Earth, through the Heart of the Earth, and through the Heart of the Cosmos, **for**

everything now is within the Heart, YOU, ALL THAT IS, embraced with pure Love in the Heart of the Creator.

It will take some time for these energies to fully imprint themselves upon the whole of the Earth Planet so that they become available to all of Humanity, But it has begun and you have performed the task that you were asked to perform, that you agreed to perform before you came to this place, and I come to thank you tonight for all the work that you have done here within Pendragon and beyond, **for each small action by an individual Light Being, or a group of Light Beings has great significance, but you will only feel the power of this Light within your Heart.**

The Blue Light of Peace, the Blue wave of Harmony are now one unified Light of Peace and Harmony, touching every Heart, embracing every Heart, becoming One with every Heart, and the Beloved Song Lines of the Earth are carrying that energy vibrantly, powerfully to every part of your Planet, and we give thanks to the Harmonics for continuing to hold the Earth in balance through this difficult time of change. **Embrace them with**

the Peace and the Harmony in your Hearts, and empower them in the work they continue to do.

Now once again focus your full attention within your Heart, open yourself and allow every Light Being of the Earth, and every Light Being of the Cosmos to <u>**BECOME THE ONENESS THAT YOU ARE**</u>.

11

SEND FORTH YOUR 'RAINDROPS OF PEACE'

October 14, 2013

(The Circle opens with the sounds of the Tibetan Bowls and the Drum.)

Relax and feel yourself moving deep into your Hearts, moving deeper and deeper into the Light within your Hearts, and allow all the discord, all the problems of your Earthly day to be dissolved by the Light frequencies deep inside your Hearts, **for it is your Hearts that guide you on this new journey into Higher Dimensional Frequencies of the Earth.**

Feel a deep sense of Peace and Harmony radiate through your Being. Breathe deeply. **Feel the Peace become the <u>essence</u> of your Being.**

Greetings Dear Hearts, I am Sananda, Cosmic Peace Ambassador. I come tonight to remind you of the **Blue Light of Peace** that was placed into your Hearts a short time ago, the **Blue Light of Peace** that is waiting to be unleashed upon your Earth, to cascade like a million raindrops across the Earth, raindrops that are so essential for new life to be created, for new growth to occur within and upon the Earth. And the time has come, as the new Light frequencies pour into the Earth from the Cosmos, the time has come to plant the new Earth with the **'Seeds of Peace'**.

You may have felt Dear Ones, that once we placed the **Blue Light of Peace** within your Heart that change would be instantaneous, but growth is sometimes slow, seeds need to be planted, and then to be nurtured, and then to be watered.

It is time now to plant the **'Seeds of Peace'** wherever you can, to allow others to feel the vibration of the **Blue Light of Peace** radiating from your Hearts, to begin to live the Peace within your Hearts, for it is only as you begin to live that Peace that it begins to flourish, it begins to grow, it begins to spread.

<u>Becoming Peace in your lives is all about intent</u>. It is about reactions to the day to day events of your lives, it is about choosing to respond to situations that occur in your lives with the energy of Peace, and not the energy of anger, not the energy of blame - **<u>the energy of Peace</u>**.

<u>Think, feel</u> and **<u>BE</u>** Peace in all situations in your lives, and yes, Dear Hearts, you will be challenged, for life is full of challenges, life is full of situations which beg you to react harshly, negatively, angrily, but if you breathe Peace with every breath you take, you diffuse those situations in your lives, and as you diffuse those situations with your radiant Peace, the causes of discomfort begin to melt away.

Send forth your 'raindrops of Peace', nurture every opportunity that comes your way to show and be the **'BEING of Peace'**.

As more and more of the Light workers on the Earth embrace the energy of Peace within their Hearts, more and more of those who are yet to awaken will begin to notice the changes of energy, and yes, at first they may wonder what this is, they may rebel against it, but in time they too will be permeated by the **Blue Light of Peace**, and they too will begin to react to the Stimulus of their Earthly lives with the response that is Peaceful and Harmonious, instead of angry and defiant.

It is fear which causes anger and defiance.

It is Love that creates Peacefulness.

Love yourselves, for when you do there will be no room for anger and defiance within you, there will only be room for Peace.

You are being asked in the near future to celebrate a day of **"Oneness"**. Oneness of what? That is the question Dear Ones. Are you going to celebrate a Oneness of anger and defiance? Or are you going to celebrate a **Oneness of Peace and Harmony and Love?**

You are all custodians of the Earth. It is up to you how you create the new Earth. Reach deep into your Hearts and take hold of the **Blue Light of Peace** and radiate it forth, gift it to every person you meet, quietly, efficiently, simply being who you are – a **Master of Peace**.

The time is now, Dear Hearts, to plant the **'Seeds of Peace'** upon the new Earth so there will be no room in the new Earth for anger and hatred and defiance, <u>**there will only be room for Peace and Love, Harmony and Oneness.**</u>

12

YOU ARE ALL AMBASSADORS OF PEACE

January 13, 2014

(The Circle opens with the sound of the Tibetan Bowls.)

Greetings, Dear Hearts, I am Sananda, Cosmic Ambassador of Peace.

I come tonight to remind you of the **Labyrinth of Divine Peace** that you walked in your Marine Meditations a number of years ago. It is time in this new year of 2014 to revisit the energies of that Labyrinth, to embrace it fully in your Hearts, to walk it again in your minds, for the **Labyrinth of Divine Peace** has a special energy projection within it.

It is the Journey within yourself to discover and create afresh the energies of TRUE PEACE in

your Heart. I know, Dear Ones, I have come many times before and spoken to you of Peace, and each time I do I seek to increase your understanding of the **TRUE** Energy of Peace. Through the Sacred Geometry of the Labyrinth you can open yourselves more and more widely to the **TRUE ESSENCE OF PEACE**, and your Planet at this time sorely needs to be reminded of the Journey that each Being must undertake to find the Peace within themselves.

Let me refresh your memories, Dear Hearts. When you enter the **Labyrinth of Divine Peace**, you move immediately to create Balance within you, Balance is essential as the first step of your Journey, you let go of all those areas of beliefs within you that are not balanced and Harmonious, and you sit and embrace the Yin and the Yang of yourself, and then, Dear Hearts, you move further on your Journey and you move into your own Heart, and you embrace the energies of **DIVINE LOVE**. You cannot find Divine Love in your Heart until you have created Balance within your Being. But when you sit inside your Heart and open it **UNCONDITIONALLY**, you **FEEL the Magic of Love as a total part of your Being.**

Once you have embraced the Divine Love within your Hearts, you then move into the **LIGHT OF THE GREAT CENTRAL SUN**, bringing into yourself the Cosmic energies of Peace, of Love, and of Harmony. **BALANCE, LOVE, AND NOW, LIGHT**. A Trinity of Energies, coming together, **FUSING** together, **UPLIFTING you**, allowing you to let go of the tendrils of fear, the tendrils of anger, the tendrils of distortion, **EMBRACING YOUR HARMONY, EMBRACING YOUR LOVE**, and now filling yourself with the **LIGHT OF PEACE.**

And then you move again to the Center of your **BEING**, and you reach deep within yourself and find the **TRUE ENERGY OF PEACE.** For do not forget, Dear Ones, walking a Labyrinth is walking into the Center of yourself, and at the Center of yourself in this **Labyrinth of Divine** Peace you begin to embrace the Peace, and you begin to understand that Peace is a **'STATE OF BEING'** - it is a **CONDITION OF LIFE** - it is **MORE** than an alternative to war.

And then, Dear, Hearts, you walk once more from the **Labyrinth of Divine Peace** and you resume your Journey upon the Earth, with a new understanding of yourself, with a new Radiance of **LIGHT**, that you **SHARE WITH OTHERS**.

So once again, Dear Hearts, I ask that in this new year of 2014 you once again embrace the **Labyrinth of Divine Peace**, and promote the **Labyrinth of Divine Peace** to others, reminding each of them who may have walked this Labyrinth with you, of the importance of this part of your Journey. You have moved through another Labyrinth since then, the **Labyrinth of INNER VISION**, and it is because you have been imbued with this new Inner Vision that you can once more revisit the **Labyrinth of Divine Peace** and see it, and experience it, with a totally different perspective of life, of the importance of **BEING THE PEACE IN YOUR HEART**.

It does not mean, Dear Hearts, that you have to lay it out on the floor and walk it again, you can do this within your Hearts and within your minds, simply embrace the energy of that Labyrinth, the **ENERGY OF THE JOURNEY TO THE PEACE DEEP AT THE CENTER OF YOUR BEING.**

For you are **NOT** Warriors, Dear Hearts,

YOU ARE ALL AMBASSADORS OF PEACE.

13

TAKE TIME EACH DAY, DEAR HEARTS, TO REACH OUT AND EMBRACE THE EARTH WITH ALL THE LOVE AND THE PEACE AND THE JOY THAT IS WITHIN YOU

April 21, 2014

(The Circle opens with the sounds of the Tibetan bowls and the bell.)

Feel the **'quickening'** and the **'awakening'** as the sound waves flow through your physical body, resonating deep within your Hearts, allowing your Heart to open like a flower, radiating forth the energies of Divine Love. And as you breathe, blow those energies of Divine Love across the face of the Earth to caress each Being of Light with the energies of Divine Love. And Feel those same energies of Divine Love being returned to you on the breeze, enveloping you into the **ONENESS** of the Earth Planet itself, feeling the Love of Gaia embracing you. **FEEL THE ONENESS**.

Greetings, Dear Hearts, I am Sananda, Ambassador of Peace, and I come to you this evening to share with you the Peace of the Cosmos, to connect through **YOU** to the Heart of the Earth Planet, bringing through the **'BLUE LIGHT OF PEACE'**, creating new Harmonic Frequencies of Divine Love, Divine Peace, Divine Joy.

It is so important at this time, Dear Hearts, to feel yourself connected strongly to the Earth Planet itself, to know that **YOUR** thoughts and **YOUR** feelings impact upon the Earth and become a part of the vibration of the Planet itself. So the importance of allowing Peace to flow through you and into the Planet is **SO** important. The Earth itself is moving through different shifts of Dimensional frequencies, and as with Humanity, it is not always at the same pace throughout, so there will be times when different parts of your Earth Planet move and shift in different frequencies, causing what you call Earthquakes and Volcanic eruptions, both on land and beneath the oceans. **These are all part of the natural process of changing environmental** frequencies, Dimensional frequencies. Just as you feel these emotional instabilities from time to time, so too does the Earth Planet.

Take time each day, Dear Hearts, to reach out and embrace the Earth with all the Love and the Peace and the Joy that is within you, and also reach out **TO** the Earth for comfort when you yourselves are going through periods of distortions of energies, Connecting, rebalancing is a **mutual** process. you are no longer separate from your Planet, you are **ALL** a part of the process of Ascension, of moving into higher frequencies of Light, **Balance and Harmony are essential components of this journey.**

As you well know, Dear Hearts, the Beloved **'Harmonics'**, that race of Universal Beings who assist Planets to hold themselves in balance through their Sound, are calling out to **YOU**, **NOW**, to embrace **THEIR** Song, to give **YOUR** energy to **THEIR** Song, so that the Earth Planet continues to be held in balance and Harmony. **This is a time of a great coming together of the Light Beings of the Earth and the Earth itself.**

The Planets of the Universe align themselves to give you the maximum energy needed for the changes that are currently underway, uplifting **YOU**, and uplifting the Earth into the Divine Love Frequencies of Light. You may, at times, feel disorientated within yourselves, or with those around you, simply recognize this, Dear Hearts, and pour more and more Love from your Heart out into the Earth, and allow the Earth to carry that vibration of Love to every other Light Being on your Planet, that **EACH** may know they **ARE** a unique and important part of the **WHOLE.**

Focus on the **'Blue Light of Peace'** that has been implanted within your Hearts, and within your higher Hearts, and when you **'Sound'**, sound forth the **'Blue Light of Peace'.** For Peace, Dear Hearts, is the Natural state of Being for **ALL** those upon your Planet, a Natural state that has been lost for eons of time, but **NOW** is ready to be embraced once more, that the Earth Planet may once again **BE** the **BLUE PLANET OF PEACE, AND HARMONY AND LOVE.**

14

WALK TALL IN YOUR PEACE, WALK LIGHTLY ON THE EARTH IN YOUR PEACE

July 21, 2014

(The Circle opens with the sounds of the Tibetan bowl, the shaker, the bell and the Blessings Chimes.)

Feel the vibrations of Love coursing through every aspect of your Being, moving out across the Earth on the waves of Sound, touching **ALL** upon the Earth, **ALL** within the Earth, and **ALL** throughout the Universe.

Greetings, Dear Hearts, I am Sananda, Cosmic Ambassador of Peace.

This may seem like an inappropriate time to come, when you are faced with so much darkness, anger, violence in different parts of your Earth, but it is,

Dear Hearts**, the most important time for me to come with my message of Peace.**

This is **NOT** the time for you to drop your heads, Dear Hearts, it is **NOT** the time for you to let go of the vision in your Hearts of an Earth filled with Peace. **NO**, it is **NOT** the time for **THAT**, Dear Hearts, **it is the time to REINFORCE your determination, your focus on your Heart, on the Peace WITHIN your Heart.**

It is time to send wave after wave of Peaceful energies out across the Earth, to send **YOUR** Light, **YOUR** Love, **YOUR** Peace, **YOUR** Harmony to all those areas of the world in turmoil.

I come tonight to ask you to stand tall, firm in your commitment to a Peaceful Earth. **That Peace begins with you**, and if you allow the darkness that you are seeing around the Earth to creep into your Hearts, the Peace will diminish within you, and because it diminishes within **YOU,** it diminishes within the rest of humanity.

In many instances at this time, Dear Hearts, you are being called upon to make judgments of others, of other's actions. It is not the time for you to be making judgments, other than the judgment of yourself. **'Am I strong in Peace?'** that is the question you must ask yourselves every moment of every day. **'Am I strong in my Peace?'** for when you embrace that strength of Peace within your Hearts and, with intent, radiate forth the power of that energy, you **WILL** create the changes necessary for the Earth Planet.

There will always be stumbles along the way, that is part of the duality of the Earth, it is part of the old vibrations still clinging to Humanity, but this is one more test for you – **'Is the Peace within your Heart real or an illusion?'**

I come to you tonight because I **KNOW,** Dear Hearts, that **the Peace within your Hearts is real, is powerful, is healing.** Ignore the calls to make judgments of others, and focus the whole of your energies on the Peace within your Hearts. **Walk tall in your Peace, walk lightly on the Earth in your Peace.** Commit yourself afresh every minute, with each breath, to the way of Peace, to the way of acceptance.

Yes, Dear Hearts, these are troubled times and your emotions are being strummed by your media. You are being asked to be angry, to be judgmental, but that is not the way. The way is to **BE PEACE**, deep in your Heart, deep in your mind, deep in your body, **BE PEACE**, for **THAT** is your contribution, Dear Hearts, to the Enlightenment of the whole of the Planet.

If each one of you refocuses your energies on the **Peace within your Heart**, changes **WILL** take place on the Earth, changes that may seem at this particular time to be unlikely will appear because **YOU** by your dedication to the energies of Peace within your Heart will be creating the necessary changes. **Resist the temptations to feel anger, to feel fear, to feel helpless.**

Dear Hearts, you are not helpless. Your Light, your energy, is what will change the Earth. So I call upon each and every one of you here tonight, and those who will hear this or read this later, move once more into that **Blue Light of Peace**, that **Blue Mist of Peace** deep within your Heart and **radiate it forth on the Sound of your breath.**

15

HOW YOU TREAT OTHERS, WITH RESPECT, WITH HONOR - THAT, DEAR HEARTS, IS WHAT CREATES PEACE UPON THE EARTH

October 13, 2014

(The Circle opens with the sounds of the Tibetan bowls and the Blessings Chimes.)

Isolate in your mind, and draw deeply into your Hearts, the Sound of the **'Blessings Chimes'**, for it represents the **New Song of the Earth**. It reminds each and every one of you of the Blessing that you are, and the Blessing you provide to others upon the Earth, your families and your friends. You **KNOW** deep within your Hearts that you are a Blessing in their lives, as they are a Blessing in yours, but all too often you allow this knowledge to fade. But

it is time now. Dear Hearts. to embrace fully the
BLESSINGS OF YOU.

Acknowledge each day the Blessings in your life,
the Blessings that **YOU** bring into your life from the
Love and the Light deep within your Hearts.

**Allow yourselves to radiate forth the Sound of
the Blessings within YOU.**

**Greetings Dear Hearts, I am Sananda, Cosmic
Ambassador of Peace** and I come tonight on the
waves of the Blessings Chimes to let you know that
there is a new wave of the mist of **Blue Light of
Peace** flowing into your Earth Planet, lifting the
vibration of Peace throughout your Earth Planet. It
will continue to flow powerfully into the Earth and
be absorbed by the Earth between now and the time
of your Solstice.

It will supplement the Sound Frequency gift that
was brought to you at the Equinox, the new **Song
of the Earth**, the **Song of Blessings**, and you will
begin to see and feel within yourself and within
others the Blessings of Peace as the blue mist flows
from deep within the Cosmos and embraces the
Earth Planet.

The youth of today on your Planet are more awakened than you were at their age, they have come to this Planet to be models of Peace and Love and Harmony, and it is significant that this has already been publically recognized by the granting of your greatest Peace Award to a child, **a child that is fighting for equality, a child that is fighting for education, but fighting through her words, through her Love, through her Heart.**

I invite you, Dear Hearts, to listen to the words of this child, to acknowledge and accept the Peace that is flowing through her into the Earth, for she is speaking to her peers, to all those other children that will be the ones who finally create the Peace upon the Earth.

Much is changing upon your Planet and much will continue to change. If you look closely you will hear and see the seeds of Peace being sown in every part your world, not upon your T.V. screens, for they still seek to influence your opinions **by showing you the worst of your world and not the best of your world,** but the influence of your T.V.'s is waning, the internet expands the opportunities for what is good upon the world to be seen and heard more frequently, but **as usual, Dear Hearts, it all begins** with the Blessings in your own Heart and how you focus those energies of LOVE, of HARMONY, of ONENESS, of PEACE and direct them out into the world.

How **YOU** treat others, with respect, with honor - that, Dear Hearts, is what creates Peace upon the Earth.

<u>Take a moment now to listen to the Blessings Chimes and absorb this message of Love, Equality, Oneness, Harmony, Joy, all those positive energies, all those positive ideas, all those positive dreams and aspirations that individuals within the collective have - and choose to focus upon.</u>

Acknowledge your own Blessedness and acknowledge the Blessedness in all others upon your Earth, for when you see the Blessedness in others you create a connection of joy between you and them, and **<u>THAT</u>**, Dear Hearts, is the building blocks of creating **PEACE ON EARTH.**

16

THAT CRYSTAL OF DIVINE PEACE IS YOUR SECOND SUN

January 5, 2015

(The Circle opens with the Sounds of the Tibetan Bowls and the Blessings Chimes.)

Imagine the Sound of the Blessings Chimes as sparkles of Light flitting hither and thither across the Earth, reaching deep into the Hearts of all Humanity, and awakening them to the Blessedness within themselves. **For it is the knowledge and acceptance of the Blessedness within each Heart that allows Humanity and the Earth to move smoothly along the pathway of Ascension.**

Each tinkle of Sound is a new Light appearing in someone's Heart. Sound and Light are interchangeable, they work as ONE to uplift, to open each and every one of you to the Divine Blessedness of yourselves.

Greetings, Dear Hearts, I am Sananda, Cosmic Ambassador of Peace.

The new Sound Frequency of the Earth shines out into the Cosmos as a brilliant **Blue Light of Peace**, for the new Sound frequencies from Arcturus contain within them the essence of Peace. The Earth has already received the **'Blue Light of Peace'** and the **'Blue Mist of Peace'**, and now it has received the **'Blue Sound of Peace'.**

Feel it vibrating within your Hearts, feel it moving out from your Hearts with every breath you take, out into the World, connecting each and every Being of Light, speaking to every Heart, reverberating throughout the Earth infusing the Songlines of the Earth and the Crystalline Grids of the Earth with the **'Blue Sound of Peace'**.

The times ahead, Dear Hearts, will be troubled at first, for the energy of Peace is a threat to those who still seek to have power over others. But their time upon your Planet is coming to an end, for the Heart is taking over from the mind, and the Heart is filled with Peace and Love. So do not be dismayed by the apparent turbulence upon your Planet at this time, look beyond – look within – **FEEL** and **HEAR** the Sounds of Peace. Look deep into your Hearts – **SOUND** deep within your Hearts – and resonate that Sound of Peace out into the World.

Remember, Dear Hearts, you are part of a greater **ONENESS,** and what **YOU** think, what **YOU** feel, what **YOU** resonate determines the Color of that **ONENESS.** When you radiate forth Love, and it joins with the energies of the Cosmos, the Blue and the Pink come together and form the Magenta waves of Peace from the Crystal of Divine Peace that sits above the Sacred Isle of Avalon. **THAT CRYSTAL OF DIVINE PEACE IS YOUR SECOND SUN!** It empowers Peace and Love upon and within the Earth. It has been awaiting **YOUR** connection, in this new Frequency of Sound, to enable it to shine forth with greater and greater power. **NOT A POWER OVER ANYONE, BUT A POWER WITHIN THE HEARTS OF EVERYONE.**

Now, Dear Hearts, imagine once more the Sound of your Blessings Chimes becoming Light Frequencies, just like your fireworks displays at your New Year's Eve, shooting up into the Cosmos.

exploding brilliant color and Light and Sound, Find that fireworks display within your own Heart, and feel how uplifted and energized you become, **YOU ARE THE ESSENCE OF THAT DISPLAY!** sending forth your Light, your Love, and most of all, **YOUR PEACE.**

Take time each day to imagine yourself as that fireworks display, showering the Earth with the beautiful colorful energies of Love and Peace, and allow the **JOY** and the Bliss within yourself to shine forth through your eyes, through your face, through your touch.

<u>WE ARE ALL ONE</u>, and we are all moving together into new frequencies of Light and Sound, for you have finally let go of the darkness and division of the past, and you have embraced the **<u>ONENESS OF ALL THAT IS</u>**.

17

HUMANS DO TEND TO THINK THEY ARE IN CONTROL OF THIS PLANET, WHEN IN REALITY THE PLANET ITSELF IS IN CONTROL OF ALL ITS INHABITANTS

May 4, 2015

(The Circle opens with the sounds of the Tibetan bowls and the Blessings Chimes.)

Be uplifted in Joy by the Sounds of the Bowls and the Blessings Chimes, focusing on the Divine Love within your Hearts enabling your Hearts to move into the highest Soul Dimension and embrace the <u>stillness</u> at the center of your Being.

Greetings, Dear Hearts, I am Sananda, Cosmic Ambassador of Peace.

I have maintained a certain distance of late, as you may have noticed. It is not because the energies of Peace have ceased to flow to Planet Earth, it is simply a recognition that the focus of many on your Planet has been of war, so to come into your midst and speak of Peace would have been a wasted energy. Humanity needs to look back and reflect and honor those who have given their lives, by **their** choice, to create a civilization that you all may be proud of, and a part of, but just as you remember the beginnings of war, it is important that you also remember the endings of war, the **declarations of Peace**, even if, Dear Hearts, in times past those declarations have not been long lasting. But **that,** Dear Hearts, was a time when the darker forces of the Earth were in complete control, and **that is no longer so.**

The energies of Love and Peace are bathing your Planet more powerfully every moment of every day and are gradually creating a more permanent energy of Peace. For this is not about the minds of humanity anymore, **it is about the Heart of the Earth,** for **it is through the Heart of the Earth that the energies of Peace will flow, and all those upon the Earth - human and non-human - will**

be touched, will be moved, will be changed by these energies radiating from within the Heart of the Earth.

Humans do tend to think they are in control of this Planet, when in reality the Planet itself is in control of ALL its inhabitants. **You see, Dear Hearts, the Earth has re-awakened to its own true purpose of existence,** it has cast aside the veils of forgetfulness that kept the Earth itself in a form of darkness, and over recent times you have all contributed to **enabling the Earth to once more become enlightened through its Heart and to begin pulsating energies of Love and Peace** through its body and out into its environment, where you as humans will gain the benefit of **TRUE Love, TRUE Peace** and **TRUE Light.**

You have, of recent times, enabled new Dimensional Frequencies of Sound to be anchored into the Earth Planet, to bring together the Crystalline Grids and the Song Lines of the Planet into a Harmonious Unity, each time a stepping stone towards the final enlightenment of the Earth itself - and this will continue, Dear Hearts. **You have, within this Circle, enabled the Blue LIGHT of Peace to be brought into the Earth**

**Planet and to be shared by all those upon the
Earth, and you have also enabled the Blue <u>MIST</u>
of Peace to envelop the Earth and filter deep into
the Earth's Heart, and <u>now the Earth is ready
to open its Heart completely, and this will take
place, Dear Hearts, at the forthcoming Solstice.</u>**

Some considerable time ago you may recall, Dear
Hearts, you were advised that the **'Crystal of Divine
Peace'** had been placed etherically over the Isle of
Avalon, the Sacred Isle of the feminine - **Avalon,
the Heart Chakra of the Earth Planet** - and that
'Crystal of Divine Peace' <u>radiated not Blue Light,
but Magenta Light</u> - the coming together of the
Blue Ray and the **Pink** Ray, the Ray of Peace and
the Ray of Love, and at the time of the Solstice that
is now to come, this Crystal will be fully activated
through all the Dimensions of the Earth Planet.
**For the Heart of the Earth is awakening fully
and completely, empowered by the Light and the
Sound that the Cosmos has been gifting to the
Earth over recent times.**

At the time we advised you of the existence of the
'Crystal of Divine Peace' we placed that Crystal
also etherically in your **'High Heart'**, so I come to
you tonight to ask you to focus your attention on

your own **'High Heart'** - the area between your Heart Chakra and your Throat Chakra. **Focus your attention, activate the 'Crystal of Divine Peace' within YOU** - between now and the Solstice - so that when that time comes and the Earth opens its Heart totally in Peace and Love you will **ALL BE** in Harmony with that Awakening, that Enlightenment, and you will help **Earth Mother** empower **HERSELF.**

All the Crystalline Grids of the Earth will pulsate with Magenta Light. The vibrational frequency of the Earth will once again be uplifted into a new Dimensional Frequency of Light and **profound changes will begin again to wash across the Earth.**

The Light Beings of the Oceans of the World will come together once more to Sing THEIR Song of Love and Peace, and you too, Dear Hearts, will Sing YOUR Songs of Love and Peace.

It will be time for Avalon to once again BE an 'OPEN CHALICE' of Peace and Love.

18

PEACE BEGINS WITHIN YOUR HEART AND MANIFESTS THROUGH YOUR ACTIONS

September 28, 2015

(The Circle opens with the sounds of the Tibetan bowls, the drum and the Blessings Chimes.)

Embrace the full moon energies, taking them deep within your Hearts, to meld with the **Magenta Light** from the Heart of Earth Mother, and open your Hearts wide to accept the inflow of the electromagnetic energies from the center of the Cosmos - **the energies of unconditional Love, the energies of Oneness** - and allow yourselves to expand your Light, connecting your Light with the Light of everyone else within this Circle and with others connecting with you at this time throughout the Earth, for at this time **<u>ALL IS IN ONENESS</u>**.

Greetings, Dear Hearts, I am Sananda, Cosmic Ambassador of Peace and I ride into your Circle tonight on the waves of energy from Source, the energies designed to empower the Earth with total Peace. Beloved Earth Mother has opened her Heart and allowed the **Magenta Energies of Peace** that she has been storing for so long, to flood out into the world, to embrace the Hearts of all Humanity and all other Beings of Light upon and within the Earth.

The essence of Oneness is alive once more upon the Earth and the new energies from source that are cascading down onto the Earth at this very moment are designed to empower **Love, Peace, Harmony and Joy**, and once these are implanted in the Hearts of all upon the Earth, great changes will take place. Humans will at last set aside their power struggles, their need to dominate and control, and instead will become as **ONE** with **unconditional Love coloring every aspect of their Beings.**

Dear Hearts, I have worked with you for a considerable amount of time, bringing different colors of Peace, different frequencies of Peace to the Earth, as the Earth has grown and is able to accept them.

As you have been told many times, there is no such thing as time beyond your third Dimension, everything happens as it is meant to happen, as your frequencies achieve a necessary level for the acceptance of new, more powerful energies.

Peace and Love are both important fundamental energies to create Harmony and Joy upon the Earth, and now they are pouring into the Earth Planet more and more powerfully every moment of every day, and each and every one of you is embracing these energies, these refined Light energies, and working with them to create the necessary changes upon the Earth.

<u>**The time of duality and separation has gone, there will be no more energies coming to the Earth Planet that will sustain the energies of duality and separation,**</u> and although they may take some time to fade within your physical Dimension, <u>**fade they will**</u>, <u>**for the energies now are of Love and Oneness**</u> **and as you open your Hearts and embrace these new energies of Love, Peace, Harmony and Joy, you will be contributing to the demise of the old energies of duality and separation, greed and control.**

Peace begins within your Heart and manifests through your actions.

You will have noticed, Dear Hearts, how there is now greater Light being shed on violence within your societies. Violence stems from duality and separation, **respect comes from Oneness, and when the energies of respect permeate throughout society violence, one against another, will also fade away.**

Yes, Dear Hearts, your newspapers and your televisions are highlighting the violence in a way they have never done before, and instead of looking at this as something to be feared, embrace it fully for the Light it is shining upon the darkness of Humanity.

This latest wave of energy from the Cosmos is connecting your minds and your Hearts, it is empowering Love, it is empowering Light. Take time to find the stillness within yourselves, allow the Love from within your Hearts to flow outwards to touch all those you meet, they too will begin to open to Love, to Oneness.

The course has been set, the train you might say is in motion, the destination is assured. Take time over these next few weeks and months to absorb the powerful energies that are coming to the Earth at this time and allow them to flow through you into the Earth to connect your Hearts with the Heart of Earth Mother.

Feel yourselves moment by moment being uplifted into a New Dimensional Frequency where Love, Peace, and Oneness dominate your Being.

19

"WE ARE HERE, WE ARE READY, WE ARE LOVE"

January 4, 2016

(The Circle opens with the Sounds of the Tibetan Bowls, the Blessings Chimes and the Drum.)

Feel the vibrations of Sound uplifting your Heart, uplifting your Spirit, uplifting your Soul, and as you do so, feel the immediate companionship of Beloved Earth Mother as she too allows the Sound vibrations to uplift her Heart, uplift her Spirit and uplift her Soul. For there is no longer, Dear Hearts, any separation between you and Earth Mother, you are both soaring into the Cosmos in a blaze of Color, Light and Sound, and you are calling out to all within the Cosmos **"WE ARE HERE, WE ARE READY, WE ARE LOVE".**

Can you feel the upliftment of those words, Dear Hearts? The Unity, the Oneness, it is so expansive, so fulfilling, so all embracing, for as you step forward on the next part of your journey you are no longer walking alone, you are walking in the embrace of Earth Mother, and you are walking in the embrace of the Creator.

Greetings, Dear Hearts, I am Sananda, Cosmic Ambassador of Peace, but tonight I come to you on this wave of Love of which you have been speaking during your meeting, for it is the energy of Love within **YOU** and within Earth Mother that will create the changes that will be taking place in the year ahead.

A time of great turmoil as all change is, but because it is Love that is creating these changes, you will no longer be cowed by the changes that take place, you will no longer retreat into fear and anger, **you will feel more and more Love and Peace within yourselves.**

I have been with you many times before, Dear Hearts, with the **Blue Light of Peace**, the **Blue Mist of Peace** and the **Crystal of Divine Peace** that sat above the Sacred Isle of Avalon and began the radiation of the

Magenta Ray from the Heart of Earth Mother. Now that radiation is at full force and I'm sure you are all beginning to see and feel the changes of **'attitude'** upon the Earth. **NOW**, Dear Hearts, to that **Magenta Light**, to that **Blue Light of Peace** and that **Blue Mist of Peace** has been added the **Purple Ray**, to create a new fusion of **Violet Flame** throughout the Hearts of everyone – Human and non Human – upon the Earth.

You are looking more and more towards the Cosmos and discovering more and more information about other Star Systems, and there will be so many more surprises in the years ahead, as you become **'knowing'** of the fact that you have never been alone in the Cosmos. That is not to say, Dear Hearts, that you will be witnessing creatures or Beings from other Planetary systems in the way that your popular media and your films have portrayed them, You will **KNOW** the **ENERGY** of Cosmic Beings, you will align with the energy of Beings from right throughout the Universe.

You will not necessarily perceive them in 'Form' - much as you would like to - for Humans have this habit of always wanting other things to look like them, so they feel comfortable, but the reality is you are **ALL** Energy Beings first and foremost. The form you have taken for this lifetime on your Planet is but a temporary phase you are moving through, but **YOUR ENERGY IS ETERNAL**, It is **OF** the Earth at this time, it has been **OF** other Planetary systems in other times. You are still the same Being, but you have had many forms, and sometimes, no visible form at all, you have simply been Light or Sound. **BUT YOU HAVE ALWAYS BEEN LOVE**, and when you chose to use a physical form on a dense Planet such as the Earth you lost your connection with the energy of Love.

That has now changed, Dear Hearts, and I am delighted to be with you to witness your **RESURRECTION OF LOVE**, for through Love you achieve Peace, and leading people – Beings – towards Peace has been the role that I, **Sananda**, have played throughout the Cosmos.

This is a time of great change, it is a time to allow yourselves to expand. Do not be afraid to embrace what comes into your lives, for nothing harmful will ever come into a Heart that is filled with Love.

Allow yourselves now to expand your Consciousness to embrace the whole of the Earth, the whole of the Cosmos, and allow your Being to vibrate with the energy of Love, and you will find that energy of Love creating **JOY** in every moment of every day, for **<u>JOY IS YOUR RIGHTFUL STATE OF BEING</u>**.

For in Joy there is no fear, there are no shadows, there are no doubts, for **Joy shines the Light of Love** and

<u>JOY GIVES BIRTH TO PEACE.</u>

20

YOU MAY CALL IT EARTH'S 'COMING OF AGE'. THE WHOLE OF THE COSMOS WILL STAND IN AWE OF EARTH MOTHER'S LIGHT AND EARTH MOTHER'S LOVE

March 14, 2016

(The Circle opens with the sounds of the Tibetan bowls, the Blessings Chimes and the drum.)

Feel the vibration of the Blessings Chimes awakening every cell of your Being, filling them with the **'Light of the Divine'**, that every part of your Being may be uplifted into your Soul Dimension Frequency and into the **ONENESS OF ALL THAT IS**.

It is important, Dear Hearts, to remember that every cell of your Being emits Sound Frequencies, so each and every one of you is a constant **'Orchestra of Sound'**, and as you breathe and as your Heart beats, you are sending out into the world the Divine Music of your total Light Being.

There is no such thing upon the Earth Planet as complete silence, for everything upon the Earth 'Sounds' with every breath it takes, with every beat of the Heart, and in this time leading up to the equinox we are asking you to be particularly aware and conscious of this fact, and to focus within your Hearts to enable the highest vibrational frequency of Light to be shared with beloved Earth Mother, for at the time of the equinox and the inflow of the **'Song of the Universe'** your Hearts will be the receptors of that song, the amplifiers of that song, and you will share it with Earth Mother.

Imagine the power of every Light Being upon the Planet singing together, the Song of their own Light Beings as well as the new 'Song of Light' from the Universe. This is not about **'doing'** anything; it is all about **'BEING'** **everything,** being the **ONENESS OF SOUND.** Every instrument within an orchestra is contained within your Being of Light, and at the time of the equinox each part of that orchestra will play its part of the melody. **Imagine how incredible that is going to be, a whole Planet and all upon the Planet and all within the Planet Sounding**

Cosmically, Sounding Spiritually, SOUNDING IN UNITY.

Greetings, Dear Hearts, I am Sananda, Cosmic Ambassador of Peace and I come to **BE** a part of your Earthly Orchestra at this very special time, for with the new **'Song of the Universe'** awakening within the Earth all the ancient energies, the original energies that came together to form this Planet, the essence of Peace will be the prevailing energy that is created.

Love and Joy will soar from every fiber of your Being as the Orchestra of your bodies Sound Forth their **melodies of Love and Joy**, embracing the energies from the cosmos, the energies of Love and Joy and Peace and Harmony from all the Planetary Systems across the Cosmos, and **beloved Earth Mother will take all this into her Heart and she will shine like she has ever shone before.**

Germain referred to it as a **'Beacon of Hope'** and that is precisely what it is, for there are many, many Planetary Systems within the Cosmos that are watching the Earth, watching to see how a Planet of such density can suddenly become a **'Planet of Light'**, and your song will move out into the Cosmos in wave after wave, after wave and it will connect with the Hearts of Beings of different Planetary Systems, different Cultures, different Life Forms, for the song is one of **HIGHEST CONSCIOUSNESS.**

We have all worked together through many life times, through many civilizations upon the Earth to arrive at this moment in time when **ALL** these energies come together as **ONE**. The Earth will be filled with such Light and such Love and you, Dear Hearts, will be an integral part of that journey. **So many Dimensional Doorways will be opened by this Light, for this Light is PURE LOVE from deep within the Heart of Earth Mother herself.**

You may call it Earth's **'coming of age', the whole of the Cosmos will stand in awe of Earth Mother's Light and Earth Mother's Love**, for no Planetary System has ever overcome such difficulties and moved from such density into such Light.

Because you are a part of the Earth you may not even see the effect this Light will have upon the Universe, but as one who travels the Universe and moves from Planet to Planet seeding the energies of Peace let me assure you, Dear Hearts, this is beyond all understanding, this is **'PURE LOVE IN**

ACTION' and I am so delighted to be a part of your orchestra at the time of the equinox - along with all your Spiritual friends, all your Ascended Masters, all your angelic hordes, for there is not one who has stepped back, **ALL** are now committed individually and collectively to this **'Explosion of Earth Love and Earth Light'.**

So, Dear Hearts, Sound your Blessings Chimes and begin the journey of Light out into the Cosmos.

21

PEACE IS TAKING ROOT IN MOTHER EARTH AND WITHIN THE HEARTS OF HUMANITY

July 1, 2016

(The Circle opens with the Sounds of the Tibetan Bowls and the Blessings Chimes.)

Feel yourself relaxing totally, letting go of all the tendrils of worries, releasing any shadows of negativity within your body, replacing them with **Light** and **Love**, Feel your Heart begin to expand, moving you slowly but surely into your Soul Dimension, where the energies of the third Dimension fall away, leaving you bathed in brilliant Light – the **Blue Light of Peace -** __Feel yourself embracing the Blue Light of Peace in your Heart.__

__Greetings, Dear Hearts, I am Sananda, Cosmic Ambassador of Peace.__

It feels different in this Circle at this time, for you have created a new energy within your Circle, a **"<u>SACRED SPACE</u>"** that uplifts your Hearts, and clears your minds, and allows yourself to draw more deeply the Peace energies into your Being.

These times of great change upon the Earth should not be viewed with fear and trepidation, they are opportunities to change the direction of Humanity and of the Earth Planet itself. For eons of time I have been visiting the Earth Planet, bringing with me different variations of Peace Energy in order to create change, and the Earth has now reached a point within that change sequence where the Peace Energies are taking hold. You will see the last vestiges of outbreaks of violence and anger upon the Earth, for these need to come to the surface in order to be released and replaced by the energies of Peace.

<u>This is a Heart based event - not an event of the mind - a HEART based event</u> – and as such it has a subtlety that is sometimes not visible to Human eyes or Human understanding, but I am here now to let you know that Peace **IS** taking root in Mother Earth and within the Hearts of Humanity, and all your Spiritual friends will be working hard and long to ensure that this **Peace Energy** germinates within the Human Heart.

Peace is an Energy just as **Love is an Energy**, it has many forms. Do not allow yourselves to be side tracked by illusions, by promises, by imagery, simply **<u>KNOW</u>** within your Heart that you are holding the seeds of Peace. Allow those seeds to germinate in your Heart and then move outwards to share with others, not as a new Religion, Dear Hearts, there have been far too many Religions that have compromised the Peace within the Heart with rules and regulations which defy Peace within the Heart. This is not about ideology, it is about simply **KNOWING** that **YOU** as Humans are basically **Beings of Peace**.

So focus on these seeds within your Heart, and share them openly, honestly, with all you meet. Do it simply by **BEING PEACE,** by **BEING LOVE**, by **<u>BEING A KNOWING PART OF THE ONENESS OF ALL THAT IS.</u>**

Beloved Earth Mother will be working with you to ensure that Peace grows and grows. So embrace Earth Mother in your Hearts, connect with the crystalline Grids of the Planet, and the Songlines of the Planet, for **ALL** are filled with Peaceful Energies.

Focus **<u>NOW</u>** on the **BLUE LIGHT OF PEACE**, and feel it filling your total Being, and

<u>"KNOW" THAT PEACE WILL PREVAIL ON EARTH.</u>

GLOSSARY

David J Adams -
"Every atom of your Being is a library of wisdom."

David J Adams websites -
http://www.dolphinempowerment.com/
MarineMeditation.htm
http://soundcloud.com/david-j-adams

Songlines – there are 12 major songlines throughout the Earth which come together at two places, Sundown Hill just outside Broken Hill in Australia (they are represented here by Sculptures) and Machu Picchu in Peru. They are vibrational, or Sound Arteries of the Planet.

Harmonics - A race of Universal Beings who assist Planets to hold themselves in balance through their Sound. There were originally 12 Harmonics holding the Earth in Balance, this changed in 2004 to 18 when the new 'Song of the Earth' came into being.

Willow Springs – Willow Springs Station is situated in the Flinders Ranges of South Australia and is a Sacred Space within which lies a confluence of the Michael and Mary Lines similar to that which exists beneath Glastonbury Tor in the UK. The two sites are energetically linked.

Blessings Chimes – A hand held instrument created from wind Chimes which are used to Bless the Earth, the Oceans and all Beings of Light upon the Earth. By going to the end of this Glossary, you can learn how to make your own Blessings Chimes.

Crystalline Grid – A structured network of Crystals throughout the Earth that are part of the electromagnetic composition of the Earth.

Isle of Avalon – A sacred Site at Glastonbury in the United Kingdom. The Glastonbury Tor is the remnant of this Island that housed the Divine Feminine aspects of the 'old Earth' religions. It continues to exist, but in another Dimensional form and is a 'gateway' to other Dimensions. It is also regarded as the **HEART CHAKRA** of the Earth Planet.

Equinox - An **equinox** is commonly regarded as the moment when the plane of Earth's equator passes through the center of the Sun's disk, which occurs twice each year, around 20 March and 23 September. In other words, it is the point in which the center of the visible sun is directly over the equator.

Solstice - A **solstice** is an event occurring when the Sun appears to reach its most northerly or southerly excursion relative to the celestial equator on the celestial sphere. Two solstices occur annually, on about 21 June and 21 December. The seasons of the year are directly connected to both the solstices and the equinoxes.

Marine Meditation – This was a Global Meditation initiated by Beloved Germain to be held at 8 pm on each Equinox, wherever people were in the world. It focused on connecting with the **CONSCIOUSNESS OF THE OCEANS**. It ran from March 1991 to September 2012 - 22 years and 44 meditations in all. See http://www.dolphinempowerment.com/MarineMeditation.htm

Crystal of Divine Peace – A massive Crystal that sits in another Dimensional frequency above the Sacred Isle of Avalon (Glastonbury Tor) in the United Kingdom. The Crystal is pulsing **Magenta** color Light. The crystal sits above the Three Fold Flame, and is pulsing its **Magenta** light **OUTWARDS** through 8 light points (8 pointed Star) and **INWARDS** through 5 light points to the Great Central Sun.

HOW TO MAKE YOUR OWN BLESSINGS CHIMES

A Blessings Chimes has a triangular wooden top, with a series of chimes dangling from it with THREE chimers of your own design. The chimes are of different sizes, thicknesses or metals to provide a variety of Tones (which we created by taking apart a number of different wind chimes) the chimes are set out in 5 rows, a single chime at the tip of the triangle, then 2 chimes, then 3 chimes, then 5 chimes and finally 7 chimes. This makes 18 chimes in all. One 'Chimer' is placed between rows 2 and 3, and then two 'chimers' are placed between rows 4 and 5.

The 'chimers' used in creating our Original Blessings Chime for the Marine Meditation were a Sea horse/sea dragon, a Unicorn, and a Dragon.

The Triangular wooden top has a small knob on it, to hold as you shake the Blessings Chime to create the vibration and resonance.

Although the original has a triangular Top and 18 chimes, you can vary this to your own intuition. The latest version that has been created for David has an Octagonal top and only 8 chimes and is called the Peace and Harmony Chime rather than a Blessings Chime to reflect it's more subtle Sound. Use your imaginations and Intuition.

Printed in the United States
By Bookmasters